TRY IT!

By Margaret Cleveland

D1508686

CELEBRATION PRESS
Pearson Learning Group

The following people from **Pearson Learning Group**
have contributed to the development of this product:

Joan Mazzeo, Lisa Arcuri **Design** | **Editorial** Betsy Niles, Donna Garzinsky
Christine Fleming **Marketing** | **Publishing Operations** Jennifer Van Der Heide
Production Laura Benford-Sullivan
Content Area Consultant Dr. Daniel J. Gelo

The following people from **DK** have
contributed to the development of this product:

Art Director Rachael Foster

Carole Oliver, Heidi Lane **Design** | **Managing Editor** Scarlett O'Hara
Pernilla Pearce, Diana Morris **Picture Research** | **Editorial** Nada Jolic
Richard Czapnik, Andy Smith **Cover Design** | **Production** Rosalind Holmes
DTP David McDonald

Dorling Kindersley would like to thank: Johnny Pau for additional cover design work.

Picture Credits: Corbis: Bettmann 7b; Jim Craigmyle 31br; Charles Gupton 6b; Ronnie Kaufmann 5b; LWA/Dann Tardif 5cr; Jose Luis Pelaez, Inc. 17tr; Michael Pole 16tr; Ariel Skelley 24tr; David Stoecklein 14; Tom Stewart 4. Julie Dennis: 23tr. Getty Images: Arthur Tilly 9b; Artur Tilly 17b; Michael Melford 13. Hulton Archive/Getty Images: Archive Photos 7tr, 8. Eha and Bernd Kern: 12b. Kathleen Marsal: 15 t,b. Newspix Archive/Nationwide News: Graham Crouch 28b; Mark Smith 29; Simon Dallinger 30. Pearson Education Inc: 17b. Reuters: 22. Serge Thorman: 28tr.

All other images: DK Dorling Kindersley © 2005. For further information see www.dkimages.com

Special thanks: Nawrose Nur, Michael Marsal and Margaret Winter, Cisco Arnold, Bonnie St. John, Madeleine L'Engle, and Jesse Martin for their inspiring stories and personal photographs

ISBN: 0-7652-5231-7

Color reproduction by Colourscan, Singapore
Printed in the United States of America
5 6 7 8 9 10   08 07 06

1-800-321-3106
www.pearsonlearning.com

Contents

computers

bowling

cooking

Go Ahead and Try It!

Remember when you first learned to ride a bike, read a book, or use a computer? At one time, all these things were new to you. Before you learned each new skill, you first had to try it. Think what you might have missed out if you had never tried!

Aren't you glad you learned to ride a bike?

There are many reasons for trying new things. People can learn about themselves and about the world. They can develop hidden, or unknown, talents, build self-confidence, and overcome **obstacles**.

Sometimes people can do new things that make the world a better place. People can build helpful inventions, run businesses, protect the environment, and make their dreams come true. This book shows how trying new things can be a fun and rewarding adventure.

▲ Have you ever tried playing a musical instrument?

▲ Acting can help build self-confidence.

Trying new activities with family or friends can make life more fun.

Discover Your Talents

Trying something new can turn an ordinary day into an exciting adventure. It can even lead to a whole new interest or uncover a hidden talent. Everyone has talents. Most people, though, have probably not discovered all of theirs. One way to uncover your special talents is to try many different activities. Sooner or later, you'll try something you're really good at.

Why not paint a picture?

Beautiful things from nature may inspire you to try a new hobby, such as photography.

Frida Kahlo (FREE-dah KAH-loh) had a special talent that she discovered in an unexpected way. When Frida was a teenager, she thought she wanted to be a doctor. Then Frida was badly hurt in a bus accident. For more than a month, she had to lie still, **encased** in a **plaster cast**. Frida didn't like lying still, and she became very bored.

Frida Kahlo

That's when Frida decided to try something new. She asked her parents for some paint and brushes. As Frida began to paint, she forgot about being bored. She realized that she really liked painting. She was very good at it, too.

Frida Kahlo painted this **portrait** as a young woman.

This is the **studio** where Frida painted.

Frida kept painting after she recovered from the accident. She had discovered a hidden talent. She had tried a new skill, and she was very successful at it. After a time, Frida became a famous painter, and people all over the world bought her paintings. This all happened because Frida was willing to try something new.

"Painting completed my life."

—Frida Kahlo

Perhaps you'll find you have a talent for painting, like Frida Kahlo. You might discover you have a talent for playing the trumpet, cooking, or repairing machines. You never know what talents you'll uncover until you give many things a try.

It's important to discover the things you're good at because doing those things makes life more enjoyable, interesting, and fun. Start out by trying new activities you think you might enjoy. Do some research on subjects you're curious about. Ask your family and friends what they like to do, and what they think you might be good at.

Have you thought about taking some music lessons?

Cooking can be fun!

9

Nawrose Nur (NAW-rohz noor) was curious about the game of chess. When he was six, he saw his parents moving figures around on a board. He thought the figures were toy soldiers. Then he realized they were part of a game. Nawrose really wanted to try this new game, so his father taught him how to play.

Nawrose Nur

Nawrose found that he loved playing chess. He played as much as he could, and soon he was very good at it. Nawrose had discovered one of his special talents. By the age of nine, he had won a gold medal and was a world champion!

If you like problem solving, you may want to try your hand at chess, just as Nawrose Nur did.

You can try something new almost anytime. Frida Kahlo had to stay in bed while she was recovering, but she still learned that painting was one of her talents. It was also something she loved to do.

Nawrose Nur was only six years old, but he discovered that he could play chess well. Before long, he was one of the best chess players in the world. This just proves that you're never too young to try something new.

If you like sports, why not try a new one?

Your Turn

★ ★ ★ ★ ★ ★ ★ ★ ★ ★ ★ ★ ★ ★ ★ ★ ★

What seems interesting or fun to you? Make a list of things to explore to discover your talents. Ask a friend or family member for suggestions, too. Your list might include various sports, games, writing, music, cooking, painting, drawing, model making, collecting, languages, photography, fixing things, or inventing new things. Then try some of your ideas! You have only your talents to discover!

Make a Contribution

You might be interested in solving a problem, improving the world, or creating an invention. First, you must test your ideas. Don't just dream about making a difference. Try it!

morpho butterfly

For example, one class of second graders in Sweden was studying rain forests. They were concerned that many thousands of trees were being cut down. Rain forests were being destroyed along with the plants and animals that live there. The children felt they had to do something to help.

These children cared enough about the Earth to help protect many acres of rain forest.

One student, Roland Tiensuu, had an idea: Maybe the class could buy some of the rain forest to save it. A scientist helped them find out how to do this. The class then asked people for donations. One person's donation could be enough to buy land the size of an athletic field! The students ended up buying many acres of rain forest in Costa Rica.

Since then, children around the world have taken up the cause and raised more than $10 million. Thousands of acres of rain forest have been saved. One class of second graders made a big difference, and it all began because someone had an idea and dared to try it.

"We knew what we wanted was important."

—Maria Karlsson, one of the students

scarlet macaw

This is part of the rain forest the children helped to save.

You might be surprised by what you can accomplish if you try. There are many ways to make a positive **contribution** to the world. Just ask Michael Marsal and Margaret Winter.

When Michael was twelve years old, he attended an ice hockey camp. He met a boy there who had a hearing loss. It was difficult for him to hear the whistle or understand instructions from the coach. Michael and his friend Margaret knew there must be other kids who had the same problem. They wondered what they could do to help.

Michael and Margaret's idea could help ice hockey players who have a hearing loss.

Margaret and Michael were only twelve years old when they invented their helmet.

The two sixth graders thought about the problem and then designed a special sports helmet. It uses flashing lights to signal athletes what to do next. Michael and Margaret won a prize for their invention. They also had the satisfaction of knowing their helmet could make life better for other kids.

What is it that you care most about? It could be something that affects many people, like saving the rain forest, or something that affects only one person, like helping an elderly neighbor carry groceries. Your idea might be to read to younger children or to organize a community clean-up day. It could be to help raise money for blankets for people in need.

the S3 Sports Signaling System

Maybe you have an idea for an invention, as Margaret and Michael did, that solves a problem. Perhaps you have an idea that requires many people to participate. Whatever your idea is, you should draw it or write about it. Then share your idea with an adult. Using your time and your talents, you can help others and make a difference.

When you work to solve a problem, something else might happen. If you help others, you may feel a sense of satisfaction. That's another reason for trying!

Your Turn

★ ★ ★ ★ ★ ★ ★ ★ ★ ★ ★ ★ ★ ★ ★ ★ ★ ★

Do you want to make the world a better place but don't know where to start? Ask a teacher or a parent for ideas. One idea is to **volunteer**. Volunteer helpers are often needed in communities. Sometimes local newspapers list volunteer activities, too. Why not volunteer to spend time with someone your age who is less abled than you?

A drawing or diagram of your idea for an invention can help others to understand it.

Learn Something New

To find out which foods, sports, games, or hobbies you might enjoy the most, you need to try them. Trying different things is an important way people learn about the world. Often, it's easier to do this with friends. Sometimes just the thought of trying something on your own is scary, but learning together with friends can be fun.

This girl is learning how to knit.

It's easier to learn new skills with friends who can show you what to do.

Trying new things from other **cultures** is a great way to learn about the world. People in different countries have their own unique traditions, holidays, foods, sports, and games. You may know about some of these already, such as karate, which comes from Asia.

Cisco Arnold

Cisco Arnold tried karate as a youth. When Cisco's dad signed him up for classes in a style of karate from Japan, Cisco wasn't at all sure he'd like it. The strange movements and white outfits were different from anything he'd ever seen. He only tried it because his dad wanted him to.

These children are learning karate.

Once Cisco tried karate, however, he couldn't get enough of it. He took class after class and learned all of the moves. He also learned about the **philosophy** and history of karate. Soon, he was assisting his teacher in class. Now, 12 years later, Cisco is a karate teacher himself.

Do you enjoy eating new foods? There are so many wonderful foods to try. Delicious food is prepared in countries around the world. If you try some, you'll go on a world tour. You could sample curry from India, lychees or lo mein from China, enchiladas from Mexico, or gado gado from Malaysia.

Read recipe books from other countries. You and your family and friends might try some of the recipes and discover some new favorite dishes. You might need to go to different stores to get the ingredients.

chicken curry from India

gado gado from Malaysia

Mexican enchiladas

Why not try some Chinese food?

How about trying a new hobby or a game from a faraway land? It can be fun to learn how people in other countries do things. For example, in Korea and Japan, the game of tag has a different twist. Children step on shadows to tag each other out.

In Israel, children play a game called Bli Yaadaim (blee yah-DAH-yeem), which means "Without Hands." Two teams stand in rows, holding a rope with both hands. One hat for each child is tossed on the floor. The first team of children to put all the hats on their heads, without using their hands, wins.

Trying Bli Yaadaim on a beach could be a lot of fun!

Trying things from other cultures teaches you about the world. It can prepare you to travel to a new place or to meet people from other countries. Learn a new language. Teach yourself the Japanese art of paper-folding, called origami. Find out how New Year's Day is celebrated in Greece or in China. What you learn about other countries and cultures may be useful someday. In the meantime, you'll have benefited by trying something new.

Dancers perform in this Chinese New Year celebration in Beijing, China.

Overcome Obstacles

People who try new things, in spite of difficult challenges, often become more sure of themselves as a result. They also have a sense of accomplishment when they succeed. If you try something challenging, you may find out that you can achieve something you didn't think you could.

Bonnie St. John

Bonnie St. John is a great example of someone who overcame a serious obstacle. When she was five years old, Bonnie's right leg had to be **amputated**. To recover, she had to do painful exercises in order to wear an **artificial** leg. Bonnie suffered through the exercises at first, but she kept doing them until she was strong enough to walk.

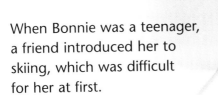

When Bonnie was a teenager, a friend introduced her to skiing, which was difficult for her at first.

When Bonnie was fifteen, she learned to ski. In two years, she was so good at it that she won a scholarship to a school for downhill ski racers. While she was at the school, Bonnie suffered two serious **setbacks**. The first was when she broke her left leg. The second was when Bonnie's artificial leg broke. "That was the lowest point in my skiing career," she said. Yet Bonnie's courage never allowed her to give up.

Don't let a disability stop you from trying.

At age nineteen, Bonnie competed in the **Paralympics**. She fell during one event, but she picked herself up and finished the course, winning a bronze medal. Bonnie won a second bronze medal and also a silver medal for overall performance.

"People fall down. Winners get up."

—Bonnie St. John

Bonnie was named the second-fastest one-legged skier in the world.

Bonnie St. John overcame a serious physical obstacle. Other people have faced different kinds of challenges. One such person is Madeleine L'Engle.

Madeleine L'Engle is a children's writer who wouldn't give up, even when other people thought she should. She knew her book, *A Wrinkle in Time*, was a good story. It shared important ideas about science and about families. Many publishers did not agree, though. One publishing company after another rejected Madeleine's book. They were sure no one would want to read it.

Madeleine L'Engle

Madeleine enjoyed reading to her granddaughters.

Madeleine has written over 60 books and is still writing.

These rejections were very upsetting to Madeleine. Still, she didn't give up. She sent *A Wrinkle in Time* to more publishers. For a year and a half, the rejections kept coming. Madeleine, though, never doubted her ability as a writer. She was sure that *A Wrinkle in Time* would be successful.

Then, one day, a publisher told Madeleine that his company would publish her book. All her hard work had paid off. Madeleine won many prizes for *A Wrinkle in Time*, and best of all, readers loved it. After this success, she was not afraid of failure.

"Be brave! Have courage! Don't fear!"
—Madeleine L'Engle

If you want to do or make something new, it can be scary. You might be afraid of failing or losing. To solve this problem, find out what is frightening about what you'd like to do. Then work out how to make your goal less frightening.

Even if you fail, it's better than not trying at all. Trying is an important accomplishment itself! Failure can be good, too, if you are able to learn something from your efforts.

Your Turn
★★★★★★★★★★★★★★★★

Do you worry what other people think about your goal? Sometimes this worry keeps people from trying new things. Remember that everyone has different likes and dislikes. Some people may feel very excited about what you're doing and others may not care at all. What should matter most is that you are trying something that's important to *you*.

Do you have a story you would like to write?

Make Your Dreams Come True

Everyone has dreams. Perhaps you want to visit Antarctica or run in a **marathon**. Maybe you want to become a pilot or study dinosaur fossils. Jesse Martin is someone who had a big dream.

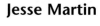

Jesse Martin

When Jesse was thirteen years old, he read a book about the adventures of a man who sailed a raft around the world. Jesse was **inspired**. He wanted to sail around the world, too. There was one big problem, though. Jesse didn't know a thing about boats!

Jesse decided to learn everything he could about boats. He studied for four years. He worked on boats, took lessons, practiced sailing safety, and interviewed sailors. By the time he was seventeen, he was ready to make his dream come true.

Jesse Martin learned how to sail so that he could sail around the world alone.

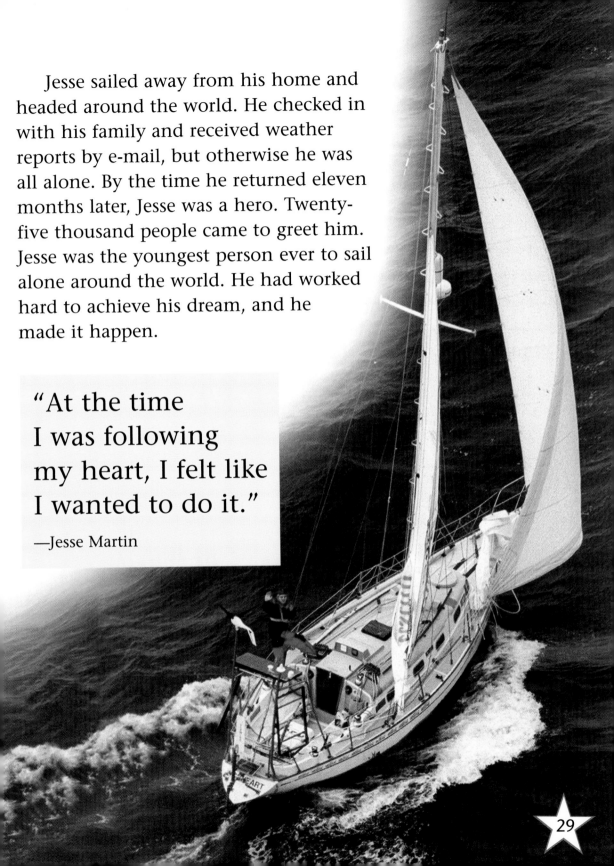

Jesse sailed away from his home and headed around the world. He checked in with his family and received weather reports by e-mail, but otherwise he was all alone. By the time he returned eleven months later, Jesse was a hero. Twenty-five thousand people came to greet him. Jesse was the youngest person ever to sail alone around the world. He had worked hard to achieve his dream, and he made it happen.

"At the time
I was following
my heart, I felt like
I wanted to do it."
—Jesse Martin

When you're working hard to reach an important goal, remember to do it safely. You should also never attempt anything that is dangerous without discussing it with an adult first. Yet, as Jesse Martin proved, you can accomplish amazing things if you're willing to prepare and work hard. Jesse will remember his trip all his life.

Your Turn

★ ★ ★ ★ ★ ★ ★ ★ ★ ★ ★ ★ ★ ★ ★ ★

If you don't have any goals in mind, now's the time to start dreaming. Talk to family members, friends, and teachers for ideas. They also might be able to help you reach your dream. Just remember, the dream is yours.

Jessie was greeted by his mother as he arrived home from his trip.

You Can Do It!

Now that you've read all the reasons to try new things, it's time to begin your own adventure. You can help others try new activities, too. Offer some encouraging words. Remind your friends of all the reasons why it's good to try something new. You can even try new things together!

Attempting new things can help you feel a sense of accomplishment. It's the best way to discover your hidden talents and interests. Trying new things can also help you make a contribution and learn about the world. It's an important step in following your dreams, too. As if that weren't enough, trying new activities can be just plain fun. So, go on and try something new!

Is ballet something you would like to do?

Face painting can be great fun with friends.

Is soccer your game?

Would you like to play the guitar?

Making up stories can be entertaining.

Glossary

amputated   to have an arm or leg cut off, usually by surgery

artificial   made by people and not by nature

contribution   the act of giving something

cultures   the ideas, customs, skills, and arts of groups of people

encased   completely covered or enclosed

inspired   guided, influenced, or motivated

marathon   a footrace that is 26 miles, 385 yards long

obstacles   things that get in the way or make something difficult to do

Paralympics   contests for athletes with disabilities that are connected with the Olympics

philosophy   the ideas or beliefs related to an activity or field of knowledge

plaster cast   a hard case that keeps a broken body part in place while it heals

portrait   a picture or painting of a person

setbacks   unexpected and often frustrating interruptions or reversals in progress

studio   a room where an artist, a photographer, or a musician works

volunteer   to choose or offer to do something because you want to